Bicycle Race

Donald Crews

Greenwillow Books,
New York

Printed in the United States of America
First Edition   10 9 8 7 6 5 4 3 2 1

Library of Congress Cataloging
in Publication Data
Crews, Donald. Bicycle Race.
Summary: The numbered order
of the twelve racers changes
as the bicycle race progresses.
1. Children's stories, American. [1. Bicycle
racing—Fiction. 2. Racing—Fiction] I. Title.
PZ7.C8682Bi 1985   [E]   84-27912
ISBN 0-688-05171-5
ISBN 0-688-05172-3 (lib. bdg.)

one

two

three

four

five

seven

six

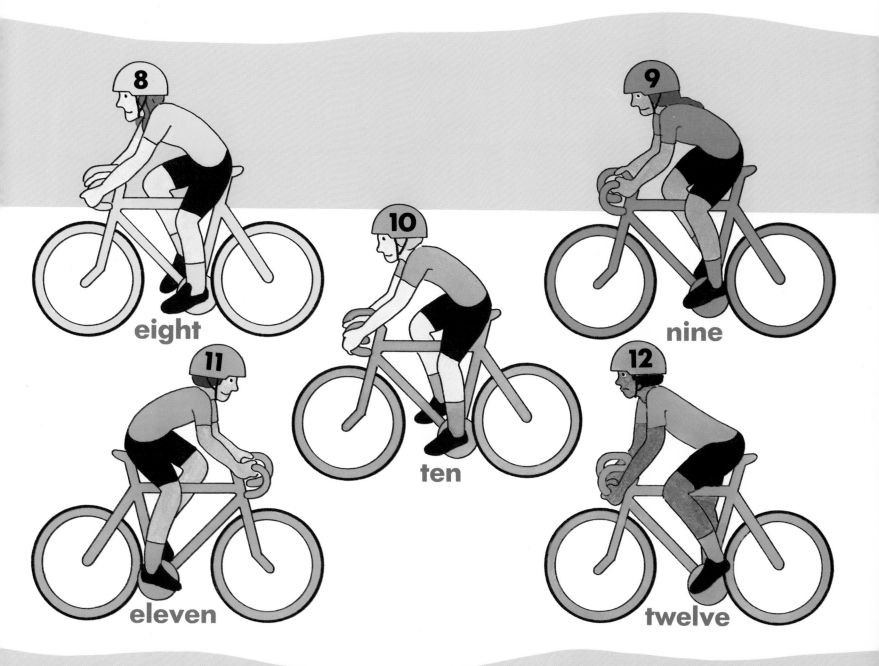

eight

nine

ten

eleven

twelve

Bicycle
race
today.

Twelve
bicycles,
twelve
riders.

R E A D Y . . .
S E T . . .

WILL O. GREEN

GO!

Number
nine is
in trouble.

WILL O. GREEN

Who's in front? Who will win?

Number
nine
needs
repair.

eight, one, three, two, ten, six, twelve,
four, seven, five, eleven

three, ten, two, twelve, seven, five, six, eight, one, eleven, four

six, three, one, five, eight, ten, seven, two, twelve, four, eleven

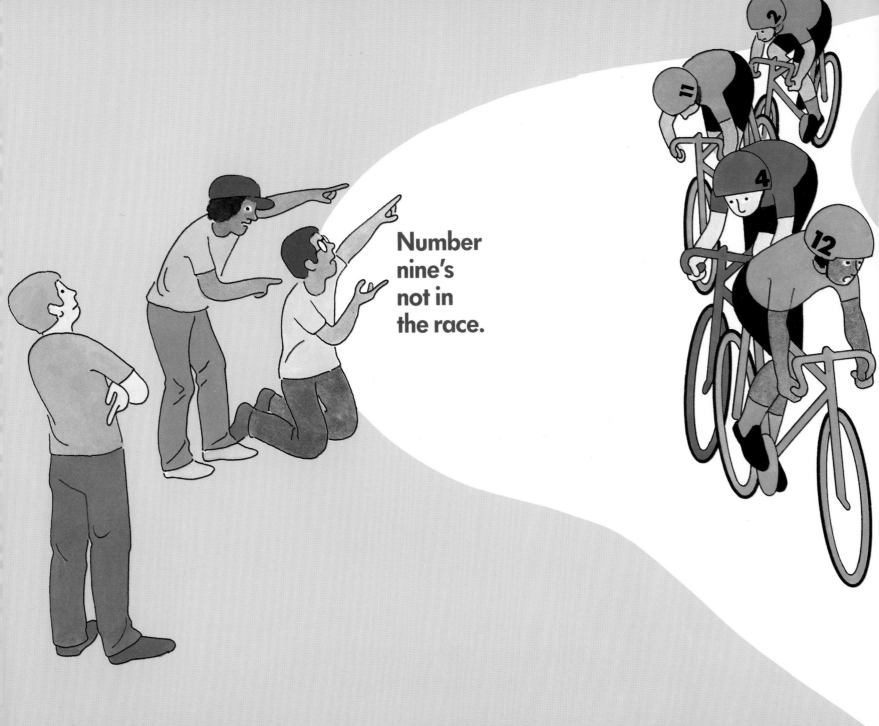

Number
nine's
not in
the race.

three, five, six, one, ten, seven, eight, twelve, four, eleven, two

one, three, twelve, five, eight, six,
eleven, ten, two, seven, four

There
she is.
There's
number
nine!

Go,
number
nine,
go!

three, six, eight, one, four, twelve, ten, five, seven, nine

Who's in front? Who will win?

six, three, two, twelve, eight,
seven, four, ten, nine, one

two,
three,
eight,
six,
ten,
twelve,
nine,
seven,
four

Here they come! Who's in front? Who will win?

ten, eight, three, nine